Don't Throw In the Trowel

Don't Throw In the Trowel

154 Practical Tips and Cheerful Quips on Gardening

TEXAS BIX BENDER

GRAMERCY BOOKS
NEW YORK

This 1999 edition is published by Gramercy Books,™
an imprint of Random House Value Publishing, Inc.,
201 East 50th Street, New York, New York 10022,
by arrangement with Gibbs Smith, Publisher.

Gramercy Books™ and colophon are trademarks of
Random House Value Publishing, Inc.

Random House
New York • Toronto • London • Sydney • Auckland
http://www.randomhouse.com/

Design: The Stiebling Group
Editor: Dawn Valentime Hadlock

Printed and bound in the United States of America

A CIP catalog record for this book is available from the Library of
Congress.

Don't Throw In the Trowel / by Texas Bix Bender
ISBN 0-517-20551-3

8 7 6 5 4 3 2 1

For Dorothy Cook Arwood

and Gertrude Caroline Arwood,

two women full of earthy insights

who never threw in the trowel.

PEOPLE WHO EAT
FROM THEIR OWN
GARDEN HAVE
GREAT TASTE.

❀

EVERYONE LIKES
TO BE TOUCHED WITH
AFFECTION — EVEN
MOTHER EARTH.

TIP NO 1

When you

pull a weed,

pull it once

and for all.

AFTER
BREAKFAST,
GARDEN A WHILE;
AFTER SUPPER,
WALK A MILE.

RATIONALIZING IS THE
ONLY WAY TO DEAL WITH
CLOVER AND DANDELIONS.
THEY FLOWER PRETTILY,
THEY BRING CERTAIN
NUTRIENTS TO THE SOIL,
AND MOST IMPORTANTLY,
THEY ARE VERY EASY TO
GROW. WHAT MORE COULD
YOU WANT?

Never refrigerate potatoes,

yams, squash, tomatoes, or pumpkins.

They hold their flavors best

at a cool room temperature.

BIG ISN'T
NECESSARILY
BETTER
IN TOMATOES OR
ANYTHING ELSE.

❀

HE WHO IS
BITTEN BY THE
"GARDENING BUG,"
GETS BITTEN BY
GARDEN BUGS.

In October

put manure in the fields.

In spring

it will increase

the yields.

IN THE SPRING
WHEN YOU ARE
PLOWING AND
PLANTING, YOU ARE
LOOKING AHEAD.
IN THE FALL
WHEN YOU ARE
HARVESTING AND
PUTTING UP,
YOU ARE STILL
LOOKING AHEAD.
THAT'S GOOD
GARDENING AND
THAT'S GOOD LIFE.

No matter
how cloudy
the sky,
it won't rain
until you water
your garden.

Plant petunias

with your tomatoes.

Petunia foliage is deadly

to several insects, including

the larvae of the

tomato hornworm.

IF YOU KEEP
AT IT, SOONER
OR LATER
YOU'LL GET YOUR
GARDEN RIGHT,
MORE OR LESS.

❁

GOOD GARDENERS
KNOW ALL
THE BEST DIRT.

There are two rules

for watering:

1. For inside plants—

when in doubt, don't.

2. For outside plants—

when in doubt, do.

PERFUMES

ARE THE

FEELINGS

OF

FLOWERS.

IN COMPARISON,
SOMETIMES A
GARDEN CAN
MAKE THE ONE
YOU LOVE SEEM
ALMOST EASY TO
PLEASE.

TIP NO 6

Never plant

more

than you can

care for.

FLOWERS AND
VEGETABLES ARE
MORTAL LIKE US.
WEEDS
NEVER DIE.

NO MATTER HOW
BIG YOU THINK YOUR
PUMPKIN IS,
SOMEONE ELSE HAS A
BIGGER ONE.

TIP NO 7

The month

of May

is when you

win or lose

your war

with weeds.

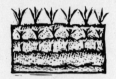

No matter
when someone
comes to
visit, your
garden looked
better the week
before.

GOOD
GARDENERS ARE
NOT NORMALLY
GIVEN TO
BRAGGING;
BUT, THEN, GOOD
GARDENERS ARE
NOT NORMAL.

TIP NO 8

Always till

one more time

before

planting.

GIVE A PLANT
TO A FRIEND AND
THEY WILL SEE YOU
IN IT AS LONG AS
IT LIVES.

NOTHING GETS A
GARDEN IN SHAPE
FASTER THAN
COMPANY COMING.

A handful of soil from your

garden holds more living organisms

than there are humans on Earth.

Their well-being

is the well-being of your garden

and this planet.

FROM TIME TO TIME,
SIT DOWN IN A
FAVORED SPOT IN YOUR
GARDEN, SIP A GLASS OF
CHILLED WINE, AND
INHALE THE SCENTS OF
GROWING THINGS.
THIS WON'T GET ANY
POTATOES PLANTED,
BUT IT WILL PEEL AWAY
A FEW CARES.

TIP №10

The best time to water

is in the

early morning

when the soil

will take the most water

to the plants.

A FLOWER IS A LIVING JEWEL.

PLANTS ARE LIKE PEOPLE — TRY AS YOU WILL, YOU JUST CAN'T GET ALONG WITH SOME OF 'EM.

TIP NO 11

Keeping a gardening

journal helps you

to avoid repeating

past sins and

mistakes.

GRASS GROWS BEST
WHERE YOU WISH IT
WOULDN'T.

EVERY YARD
SHOULD HAVE A FEW
OLD FRIENDS THAT POP
UP WITHOUT WARNING
AND BLOOM WHEN
MOST NEEDED.

The best way to be happy with
your flower garden is to draw up an
elaborate plan that blends pastels
perfectly, contrasts vivid blooms
dramatically, and interweaves showy
magnificence with subtle beauty—
yeah, right!

DON'T LET
BEGINNER'S LUCK
GIVE YOU
DELUSIONS OF
KNOWLEDGE.

YOUR GARDEN
IN THE SPRING
IS NEVER AS BIG AS
IT WAS WHEN YOU
PLACED YOUR SEED
CATALOG ORDER
LAST
WINTER.

Feed the soil,

not the plant.

OLD AMISH SAYING

ANYBODY WHO THINKS
THAT GARDENING
BEGINS IN THE SPRING
HAS WASTED THE FALL
AND WINTER.

EVERY
GARDEN
BEGINS WITH
A DREAM.

When mulching around a tree,

don't use uncomposted materials.

While the materials break down,

instead of adding nutrients to the soil

they leech them away.

A GARDEN IS

A THING OF BEAUTY,

AND A

JOB FOREVER.

A GOOD GARDENER

KNOWS HIS

LIMITATIONS BUT

ISN'T CONFINED

BY THEM.

Dig up twice

as much space

and plant half

as many vegetables

as you think you'll

need.

YOU CANNOT
UNDERSTAND A
GARDEN UNLESS
IT HAS SOILED
YOUR HANDS.

NATURE IS NOT
NECESSARILY SMARTER
THAN YOU, BUT SHE
DOES KNOW MORE
THAN YOU DO.

TIP NO 16

Never spend

a fortune on tools

that you

chronically lose.

GARDENING IS A
DAY-TO-DAY ENDEAVOR.
IF ONE DAY GOES BY
WHEN YOU DON'T
AT LEAST WALK OUT
AND LOOK AT YOUR
GARDEN, COUNT ON
A MINIMUM OF TWO
DAYS TO GET IT
BACK IN GOOD FORM.

GATHER YE
ROSEBUDS WHILE
YE MAY,
OLD TIME IS
STILL AFLYING:
AND THAT SAME
FLOWER THAT
SMILES TODAY,
TOMORROW WILL
BE DYING.

Robert Herrick 1591–1674

TIP NO 17

You can't use simple addition

and subtraction to figure out

how to grow your garden.

What adds up to good health

for one plant

can easily take away

from the health of another.

YOUR IDEA OF
A GARDEN IS
THE BEST GARDEN
FOR YOU.

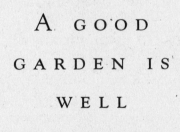

A GOOD
GARDEN IS
WELL
GROUNDED.

TIP № 18

Instead of bagging those fall leaves

and setting them by the curb,

put them on your garden

and till them into the dirt.

As a soil builder,

they can't be beat.

IN SPITE OF
ALL THE TIMES
A MORTAL
TILLS THIS
EARTHLY COIL,
A WEED'S SEED
OR SNIP OF ROOT
IS ALWAYS
LURKING IN
THE SOIL.

READING GARDEN
CATALOGS IN THE
WINTER IS LIKE
HAVING COCKTAILS
IN THE EVENING:
AFTER ONE OR TWO,
YOUR BIG PLANS
BEGIN TO LOOK
FEASIBLE.

Hot tip for tomato lovers:

According to the U.S. Department

of Agriculture, hairy vetch

will increase your tomato harvest

by 138 percent!

(Hairy vetch is a ground cover that

adds nitrogen to the soil.)

A GARDEN IS NATURE'S SUPERMARKET.

NOTHING IN THE WORLD REFLECTS THE CHANGES OF NATURE BETTER THAN A GARDEN.

An inch of water will

moisten clay soil to a

depth of six inches.

It will moisten sandy soil

twelve inches, and loamy soil

nine inches.

IF YOU WANT TO
BE HAPPY FOR AN HOUR,
DRINK WINE.
IF YOU WANT TO
BE HAPPY FOR A DAY,
RUN AWAY.
IF YOU WANT TO
BE HAPPY FOR A YEAR,
GET MARRIED.
IF YOU WANT TO
BE HAPPY FOREVER,
BE A GARDENER.

Ancient Greek Saying

GARDENERS ARE
UNDENIABLY
"NUTS."
IT PROBABLY
COMES FROM
STEPPING ON
THEIR RAKES,
TINES UP, TOO
MANY TIMES.

TIP №21

Watering for

ten minutes in the

early morning does

as much good as

watering for an hour

in the afternoon.

A HOUSE WITHOUT
A GARDEN IS A
TEMPORARY HOME.

A GARDEN
IS A PLACE WHERE
YOUR MIND GOES
TO SEED.

TIP NO 22

Petunias don't like

water on their flowers.

Rain or overhead watering

causes them to close up

for two or three days.

IF WEEDS COULD
THINK, THEY WOULD
HAVE BEEN ON THE
MOON LONG BEFORE
NEIL ARMSTRONG.

A GARDEN IS A
SUBLIME LESSON
IN THE UNITY OF
HUMANS AND
NATURE.

Never work soil or walk

on soil when it is wet.

By doing so, you close

tiny circulation passages that are

vital to the soil's health.

The result is hard, lifeless clods.

A GARDEN GROWS
MORE THAN JUST
FLOWERS AND
GOOD THINGS TO
EAT; IT ALSO
GROWS BOUQUETS
OF KIND THOUGHTS
AND BUSHELS OF
CONTENTMENT.

TO OWN A BIT OF
GROUND, TO SCRATCH
IT WITH A HOE,
TO PLANT SEEDS AND
WATCH THE RENEWAL
OF LIFE — THIS IS THE
COMMONEST DELIGHT
OF THE HUMAN RACE!

Charles Dudley Warner, 1829–1900

TIP NO 24

To find out if your soil

is ready to be worked,

take a handful and compress it.

If it turns into a sodden lump,

it's too wet.

If it's soft and crumbly, it's ready

to be turned and tilled.

ONE WHO
GROWS DOES NOT
GROW OLD.

IF YOU WOULD BE HAPPY
FOR A LIFETIME, PLANT
A GARDEN — ALL RIGHT,
MAKE THAT BUSY FOR
A LIFETIME.

While cabbage

is still growing,

sprinkle a little table salt

on each head

to keep worms away.

GARDENERS HAVE
SOAKER HOSES
RUNNING THROUGH
THEIR BRAINS.

MOTHER EARTH
IS SO GIVING,
IF YOU MERELY TICKLE
HER WITH A HOE
SHE LAUGHS OUT
A HARVEST.

TIP №26

The best cure

for backache

is a longer handle

on your hoe.

A GARDEN
IS THE
ONLY WAY TO
TRULY EAT
THE FRUITS OF
YOUR LABOR.

Never borrow

a garden tool unless

you know how to use it;

never use it

unless you know

how to take care of it.

A GARDENER
IS A PRODUCER;
ANYONE ELSE
IS JUST A
CONSUMER.

THE BEST WAY
TO GARDEN IS TO PUT ON
A WIDE-BRIMMED STRAW
HAT AND SOME
OLD CLOTHES,
AND WITH A HOE IN
ONE HAND AND A COLD
DRINK IN THE OTHER,
TELL SOMEBODY ELSE
WHERE TO DIG.

TIP Nº28

The best thing

you can do

after working

in your garden is

to clean your tools.

GARDENING IS
A GROWING
EXPERIENCE.

TO PLANT IS TO
LOVE OTHERS
BESIDES ONESELF.

Old English Proverb

Tip №29

For a head start in the spring,
turn your garden in the fall and leave
it alone through the winter. This will
aerate the soil, allow it to better soak
up moisture, and will cause it to heat
up faster in the spring, pushing your
first picking ahead by
as much as three weeks!

FLOWERS ARE
THE SWEETEST
THINGS GOD
EVER CREATED
AND FORGOT TO
PUT A SOUL
INTO.

Henry Ward Beecher, 1813–1887

A GOOD GARDEN IS
THE TRIUMPH OF HOPE
AND EXPERIENCE —
EVERY YEAR YOU HOPE
YOUR GARDEN WILL
TURN OUT WELL, BUT YOUR
PAST EXPERIENCE TELLS
YOU BETTER.

TIP NO 30

The best time

to cut roses

is just before

their petals open,

in the A.M. before

the sun hits them.

THERE ARE THOSE
WHO THINK OF
GOLDENROD AS A FLOWER AND
THOSE WHO THINK OF
GOLDENROD AS A WEED.
THERE ARE THOSE WHO DON'T
THINK OF
GOLDENROD AT ALL.
A GARDENER THINKS,
A GARDENER
UNDERSTANDS, AND
A GARDENER KNOWS
WHAT TO CALL IT.

NOTHING
IS MORE
COMPLETELY THE
CHILD OF ART THAN
A GARDEN.

Sir Walter Scott, 1771–1832

Like children,

mint will get into anything,

so be careful

where you plant it.

GARDENERS
HAVE THEIR ROOTS
IN THE EARTH.

THE LEAST
EXPENSIVE LAWN
MOWER YOU CAN HAVE
IS SEVEN SHEEP
TO THE ACRE.

The less water you give

a hot chile, the hotter it will be.

The more water you give

a sweet chile, the sweeter it will be.

The closer any chile is

to the bottom of its plant,

the more pungent it will be.

IF YOU EVER
GET LOST IN THE
OUTDOORS,
START DIGGING A
GARDEN. BEFORE YOU
GET THE SECOND
SPADEFUL OF EARTH
TURNED, SOMEONE WILL
COME ALONG AND SAY,
"WHAT'CHA DOING
THERE? THAT AIN'T NO
WAY TO DIG
A GARDEN."

THE WONDER OF
A GARDEN IS HOW
IT CAN EAT UP YOUR
TIME AND ENERGY
WITH SIMPLE
APLOMB AND THEN,
IN A WEEK OR TWO,
GIVE YOU BACK
A SIMPLE BLOOM...
OF COURSE, TO A
GARDENER THERE IS
NO SUCH THING AS
A SIMPLE BLOOM.

Tilling at night will help keep

weeds out of your garden.

When you till you turn up weed seeds

and re-bury them as you go.

If they never see the light,

the seeds will never germinate.

THE REAL
LOWDOWN ON
GARDENING
IS ... DIRT.

❋

A WATCH IS NO GOOD
IN A GARDEN, WHERE
THE TIME TO DO
THINGS IS WHEN THEY
NEED TO BE DONE.

Mulching around your trees

conserves soil moisture,

prevents erosion,

and protects the root ball

against freezing.

SURPRISE GIFTS FROM
MOTHER NATURE
WITHOUT WARNING
DO APPEAR.
A PLANT YOU NEVER ASKED
FOR CAN BE A WELCOME
VOLUNTEER.
BUT WEEDS YOU NEVER
DREAMED OF
AND THAT BRING YOU NO
GREAT CHEER,
IN HER KIND AND
GIVING MANNER
SHE'S ALSO SENDING
YOU THIS YEAR.

TIP N^O35

A sure way to get the garden soil
off your hands and out from under
your fingernails is with denture
cleaner (the tablet kind that fizz
when put in water). Wet one, take
a little fizz from it, work it under your
nails and over your hands, then
wash it off with soap and water.

ETERNAL VIGILANCE
IS THE PRICE OF A
HEALTHY GARDEN.

❊

MOST WEEDS ARE
JUST LOOKING FOR A
LITTLE PLACE
TO CALL HOME.
CRABGRASS,
ON THE OTHER HAND,
HAS A HIDDEN AGENDA.
IT'S OUT TO TAKE
OVER THE WORLD.

TIP №36

To preserve cut flowers,

use a tablespoon

of Listerine per

one quart of water.

THE BEST TIME TO
PLANT A TREE WAS
TWENTY YEARS AGO.
THE NEXT BEST
TIME IS NOW.

JUST BECAUSE
YOU GARDEN
DOESN'T MEAN YOU
HAVE TO LOVE
EVERY BLASTED PLANT
THAT COMES ALONG.

TIP NO 37

Basil picked at the end

of the day keeps twice

as long as basil

picked in the morning.

YOU CANNOT
MEASURE SUCCESS IN
A GARDEN BY ANY
ACCOUNTING METHOD
OTHER THAN PERSONAL
SATISFACTION.

❀

GARDENERS ARE
THE ONLY ONES WHO
TRULY HAVE
"FLOWER POWER."

TIP Nº38

Soil with earthworms is not

only richer than soil without them,

but the higher the number

of earthworms per square foot,

the faster the absorption rate

of water—up to sixty times faster.

WHAT IS A WEED?
A PLANT WHOSE
VIRTUES HAVE NOT YET
BEEN DISCOVERED.
Ralph Waldo Emerson, 1803–1882

WHAT IS A WEED?
A PLANT WHOSE
VIRTUES DO NOT
EXIST.
Texas Bix Bender

THE
BENEVOLENT
INDIFFERENCE
OF NATURE
IS BOTH A
GARDENER'S
BANE AND JOY.

TIP NO 39

The best way to increase

the number of night crawlers

in your garden is to

mulch with leaves

or grass clippings.

A GREEN PLANT
GETS 90 PERCENT
OF ITS NUTRIENTS
FROM THE AIR AND
10 PERCENT FROM THE
SOIL; ATMOSPHERE IS
SO IMPORTANT WHEN
DINING.

THE HARDEST PART
ABOUT GOING THROUGH
A SEED OR NURSERY
CATALOG IS DECIDING
WHAT NOT TO ORDER.

A plant that flowers

before its roots

are firmly established

will seldom be

strong and healthy.

YOU CAN BUY
ALL SORTS OF
DANDY-LOOKING
OUTFITS TO GARDEN IN,
BUT THE TRUTH IS,
YOU ARE BOTH
POLITICALLY AND
FASHIONABLY
CORRECT TO WEAR
WHATEVER THE BLAZES
YOU WANT TO.

SOMETIMES
PLANTS JUST WON'T
GROW WHERE
YOU ARE.
IF YOU MOVE,
HOWEVER,
THEY'LL GROW
WHERE YOU WERE.

TIP №41

The first thing any gardener needs

to learn is not to get carried away

buying trees and plants.

The more money you spend, the

more money you'll lose and the

more brokenhearted you'll be if your

purchases don't survive.

THE WAY TO A
GREEN THUMB IS
THROUGH DIRTY
FINGERNAILS.

GARDENERS GET
DOWN TO EARTH
AND THEN SOME.

TIP NO 42

Using markers to

label what you've planted

will help you to

keep it all straight

but won't lead to

any fun surprises.

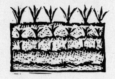

A GARDEN

IS

LIVING ART.

A LOT OF GARDENING
IS JUST COMMON SENSE.
FOR INSTANCE,
L. RON HUBBARD
(YES, *the* L. RON HUBBARD)
ONCE HOOKED UP A
LIE DETECTOR TO A
TOMATO PLANT AND JABBED
THE PLANT WITH A NAIL.
ACCORDING TO RON,
THE PLANT REGISTERED
A STRONG DISLIKE FOR
THIS KIND OF TREATMENT.
NO KIDDING.

TIP N0 43

Don't put too much

faith in weather forecasters—

all they're giving you

is their best guess.

IF YOU PLANT,

YOU GROW.

IN

A QUIET WAY,

GARDENING

IS WAR.

TIP NO 44

Corn wilts noticeably

when it needs water.

Tomato plants and cucumbers

turn their lower leaves a

deeper shade of green

when they get thirsty.

THE REAL
UNDERLYING
DIFFERENCE BETWEEN
A GARDENER AND A
NON-GARDENER
IS HOW THEY VIEW
EQUINE FECES.
TO A GARDENER
IT IS FERTILIZER.
TO A
NON-GARDENER
IT IS
HORSE POOP.

THERE ARE BUGS
FROM WHICH YOU COWER,
THERE ARE BUGS
YOU SQUEEZE WITH EASE,
THERE ARE BUGS
THAT BUGS DEVOUR,
THERE ARE BUGS
THAT BITE YOUR KNEES,
THERE ARE BUGS
YOU HATE WITH PASSION,
THERE ARE BUGS
AT WHICH YOU SCOFF,
BUT THE BUGS
THAT EAT YOUR FLOWERS
ARE THE BUGS
THAT TICK YOU OFF.

Pumpkin jack-o'-lanterns

are rich in nitrogen

and make great

post-Halloween

additions to the

compost pile.

GARDENERS LOVE
TO SHARE . . .
ESPECIALLY ADVICE
AND CUCUMBERS.

WEEDS ARE
CRACK ADDICTS.
NO MATTER HOW SMALL
THE CRACK, THERE'S A
WEED THAT DESPERATELY
WANTS IT.

Whatever kind of plant it is,

if the stem has bark,

it shouldn't be pruned or fertilized

until it goes dormant.

You can usually tell it's dormant

when the leaves fall off.

THE FASTEST-GROWING
THING IN YOUR
GARDEN IS AN OKRA
POD OR A ZUCCHINI
YOU THOUGHT
WAS NOT QUITE BIG
ENOUGH TO PICK
YESTERDAY.

IT'S A
BUG-EAT-BUG
WORLD.
(AND IT'S A
BUG-EAT-
GARDENER
WORLD.)

TIP NO 47

Every little weed

you pull in the fall

is one big weed

you won't have to pull

in the spring.

A GARDEN EXPERT
IS ANY ORDINARY
PERSON TALKING
ABOUT SOMEBODY
ELSE'S GARDEN.

THE SECRET TO
GARDENING IS TO
BUY BY THE OUNCE
AND PICK BY
THE BUSHEL.

TIP NO 48

The one-cent solution to

keeping cut tulips from

opening too far and

losing their chic tulip shape

is to drop a penny

in the water.

FEW THINGS ARE HARDER
TO ENDURE THAN A
LUCKY GARDENER:

● "I JUST PUT THE SEEDS
IN THE GROUND AND GOT A
FIFTY-POUND TOMATO."

● "YOU EVER SEEN A
WATERMELON THIS BIG?
DIDN'T FERTILIZE IT ONCE."

● "I THREW AN APPLE
CORE IN THAT PILE OF LEAVES
LAST FALL AND LOOK AT THAT
ORCHARD I GOT NOW."

G ARDENERS

RAISE CORN,

NOT HELL.

TIP №49

If you don't get

an inch of rainfall a week,

you need to

water your garden.

WATER IS
FRESHEST AT ITS
SOURCE, AS ARE
VEGETABLES, FRUITS,
AND FLOWERS.

SOMEBODY WHO'S
ALWAYS BRAGGING
ABOUT WHO HE'S
DESCENDED FROM IS
LIKE A POTATO,
THE BEST PART
OF WHICH IS
UNDERGROUND.

TIP №50

The three biggest threats to the life
of a tree are human-borne:
1. An intentional threat is the
use of a chain saw.
2. An unintentional threat is using a
string trimmer too close to the tree—
this creates scrapes and breaks in
the bark which can lead to a
variety of problems.
3. A well-meaning threat is mulching
too heavily and too close to the trunk.
This can cause crown rot and
encourage insect attack.

If you lived in the desert, which would you rather have—an oil well or a garden? In certain parts of Saudi Arabia, a gallon of gasoline costs 41¢ and a watermelon costs $21!

SELDOM DOES A
NURSERY CATALOG
DESCRIPTION LIVE
UP TO THE
REALITIES OF
YOUR GARDEN.

NO MATTER HOW
BIG OR SMALL
A GARDEN IS,
THERE IS NEVER
ENOUGH TIME TO GET
EVERYTHING DONE.

TIP №51

Better to have a small,

well-tended garden

than a large,

overgrown

patch of weeds.